Piano Sketches
Duets

Vitalij Neugasimov

Book 1

6 easy pieces for piano four-hands

MUSIC DEPARTMENT

OXFORD
UNIVERSITY PRESS

Great Clarendon Street, Oxford OX2 6DP,
United Kingdom

Oxford University Press is a department of the University of Oxford.
It furthers the University's objective of excellence in research, scholarship,
and education by publishing worldwide. Oxford is a registered trade mark of
Oxford University Press in the UK and in certain other countries

First published 2017

Impression: 1

ISBN 978-0-19-351765-3

Music and text origination by Katie Johnston

Printed in Great Britain on acid-free paper by
Halstan & Co. Ltd, Amersham, Bucks.

*Thank you so much to my sister Liudmila Neugasimova, an exceptional piano teacher,
for her invaluable contribution, brilliant ideas, encouragement, and support.*

Contents

Performance, backing and practice tracks are available on the Companion Website: www.oup.com/pianosketchesduets.

Durations are given below each piece.

Raindrops in the Morning

Vitalij Neugasimov

Raindrops in the Morning

Vitalij Neugasimov

Duration: c.2 mins

Wind of Spring

Vitalij Neugasimov

Wind of Spring

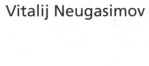

Vitalij Neugasimov

Duration: c.1.5 mins

Just for You

Vitalij Neugasimov

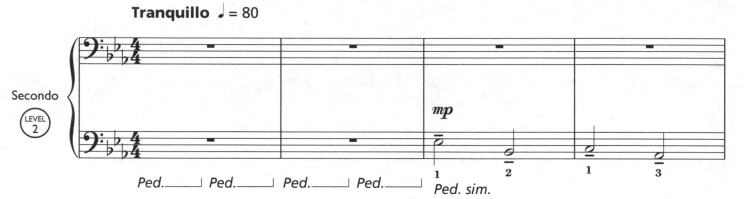

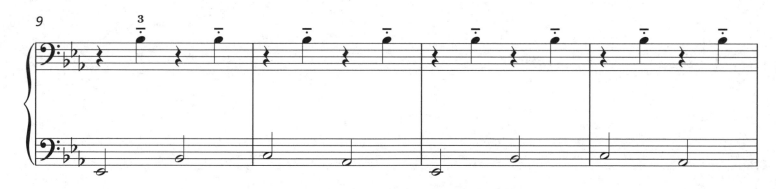

Just for You

Vitalij Neugasimov

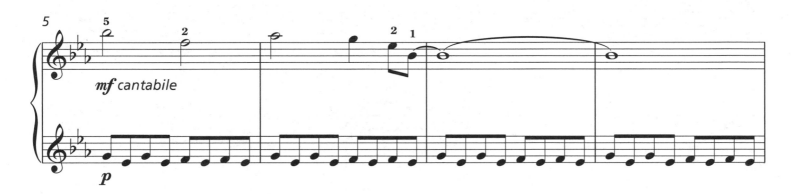

Duration: c.3 mins

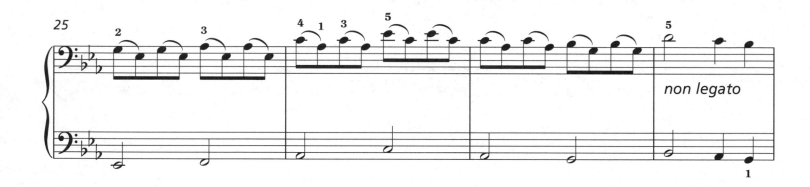

High in the Sky

Vitalij Neugasimov

High in the Sky

Vitalij Neugasimov

Duration: c.1.5 mins

Crazy Clown

Vitalij Neugasimov

Crazy Clown

Vitalij Neugasimov

Duration: c.1.5 mins

The Glorious Pastime

Vitalij Neugasimov

The Glorious Pastime

Vitalij Neugasimov

Duration: c.2 mins